Unrealistic Expectations

Navigating Advance Directives and Healthcare Decisions

Jacob Paige, R.N.

Disclaimer

Remember, this book serves as a guide. Seek professional advice, consult with healthcare providers, and consider individual circumstances in order to make the most informed decisions.

Copyright © 2024 by Jacob Paige
All rights reserved.
No portion of this book may be reproduced in any form without written permission from the publisher or author, except as permitted by U.S. copyright law.

"To cure sometimes, to relieve often, to comfort always."

— Hippocrates

Dedicated to the Entire Team of Healthcare Professionals. This book is dedicated to each of you who tirelessly devote your skills, compassion, and expertise to saving lives and improving patient outcomes. From the steadfast doctors and nurturing nurses to the meticulous pharmacy technicians, compassionate respiratory therapists, diligent lab technicians, skilled EKG techs, and efficient unit secretaries—your unwavering commitment forms the backbone of exceptional patient care.

To the palliative care teams and hospice caregivers who provide comfort and dignity in challenging times, and to the empathetic Chaplaincy, social workers, and dedicated case managers who navigate complex healthcare journeys with compassion and advocacy, your contributions transcend treatment to touch lives profoundly.

I cannot and will not leave out dietary, EVS, central supply, and facilities workers. You all make an unseen and always unrecognized difference.

Your selflessness, resilience, and unwavering dedication inspire us all. This book celebrates your invaluable role in healthcare and recognizes the profound impact of your teamwork, expertise, and humanity on patients and their families.

With deepest gratitude and admiration,
JP The RN

TABLE OF CONTENTS

Prologue: Honoring Their Wishes 9
Chapter 0.5: How to Use This Book 11
Chapter 1: Advance Directives 15
Chapter 2: Doing my job (advocacy) 19
Chapter 3.0: Unrealistic expectations 25
Chapter 3.1: The team 27
Chapter 3.2: The team in action 31
Chapter 3.3: It's time 35
Stories from the frontline 38
    Mary BSN- ICU Nurse 12 years 38
    Amanda BSN, RN, CWS, CCRN - ICU Nurse 41
    MIRANDA, BSN, MSN 46
Chapter 4: The Toll it takes 49
Chapter 4.5: The Legal dilemma: physicians, Advance Directives, and the fear of lawsuits 55
Chapter 5: Understanding Palliative Care 61
Chapter 6: Understanding Hospice Care 65
Chapter 7: Subjective thoughts from those who do 69
Chapter 8: The Importance of Having a Difficult Conversation 71
The Checklist 74
About the Author 84

PROLOGUE

Honoring Their Wishes

In the quiet corridors of a hospital, amidst the hum of machines and the soft tread of weary footsteps, a profound silence often lingers—a silence pregnant with unspoken hopes and fears, decisions that carry the weight of a lifetime, and the tender ache of love in its purest form.

This book is born from the understanding that within each of us lies a wish to live with dignity, be heard even in our silence, and depart this world surrounded by the peace of our choices. It speaks to the heart of what it means to honor those we love—not just in life, but in those moments when life hangs in the balance.

For too many families, the sudden onset of a medical crisis thrusts them into a realm where decisions must be made swiftly, often without the guidance of the person they hold most dear. In these moments, the importance of Advance Directives—those quiet documents frequently tucked away until they are desperately needed—becomes starkly apparent.

Imagine a daughter sitting beside her mother's bedside, grappling with the agonizing choice of whether to continue life-saving measures. The monitors beep insistently, a symphony of urgency, while memories of shared laughter and whispered confidences flood her mind. In that pivotal moment, she finds solace not in her uncertainty but in the clarity of her mother's wishes, spelled out in meticulous detail within her Advance Directives.

This book seeks to illuminate the path toward such clarity, urging us to engage in conversations that transcend discomfort and embrace compassion. It calls upon us to speak the words "I love you" with the fullness of their meaning, not just in moments of joy but as a beacon that guides us through life's inevitable transitions. By doing so, we gift our loved ones with our affection and the profound assurance that our love is boundless enough to respect their deepest desires.

Through stories and reflections, this book invites you to ponder what it means to honor a loved one's autonomy and dignity—to understand that the ultimate act of love may lie not in clinging desperately to life at all costs but in gracefully relinquishing control when the time comes. It is a call to action, a plea to engage in the delicate dance of preparation and acceptance so that when the hour of parting arrives, it is not met with frantic decisions made in fear but with a gentle reverence for a life well-lived and a legacy of love enduring beyond words.

As you journey through these pages, may you find comfort in knowing that by honoring their wishes, you celebrate the essence of who they are—a beloved soul whose presence has shaped your world in ways both seen and unseen. Together, let us embrace the profound responsibility of respecting Advance Directives and saying "I love you" with sincerity, ensuring that when the time comes to bid farewell, it is a moment of quiet grace guided by love, understanding, and unwavering respect.

CHAPTER 0.5

How to Use This Book

Welcome to a journey that delves into the essential aspects of healthcare advocacy and the pivotal role of nurses in patient care. This book is designed as a resource hub, drawing insights from real-life stories, expert advice, and practical guidance to empower you to navigate critical healthcare decisions and advocate effectively for yourself and your loved ones.

Navigating the Content

1. **Understanding Advance Directives**: Explore chapters dedicated to understanding Advance Directives. Learn how to articulate your medical preferences and ensure they are honored, empowering you to control your healthcare decisions even in challenging circumstances.

2. **Nurse Advocacy**: Dive into narratives and strategies highlighting nurses' indispensable advocacy role. Discover firsthand how nurses go above and beyond to safeguard patient rights, ensuring compassionate care and meaningful outcomes.

3. **Practical Advice and Calls to Action**: The book contains actionable steps and practical advice

interspersed throughout. These sections provide tangible tools and resources for initiating crucial conversations, navigating healthcare systems, and advocating effectively for yourself or your loved ones.

4. **Stories from the Frontlines**: Gain insights from poignant stories shared by nurses, managers, physicians, social workers, and other healthcare professionals who have witnessed and championed transformative patient experiences. These narratives illuminate the profound impact of advocacy and compassionate care in healthcare settings.

Applying What You Learn

Reflection and Application: After each chapter, consider how the insights resonate with your healthcare journey. Consider how you can apply newfound knowledge to advocate more effectively for yourself or support others in making informed decisions.

- **Action Steps**: Utilize the actionable steps and checklists to engage in healthcare planning and advocacy proactively. Whether completing an advance directive, initiating conversations with healthcare providers, or advocating for policy change, every action counts toward empowering yourself and others.

Engaging Beyond the Book

- **Community and Support**: Join communities or engage with organizations dedicated to healthcare advocacy and patient rights. Connect with others who share similar experiences and learn from their journeys of navigating healthcare challenges.

- **Advocacy Beyond Borders**: Explore opportunities to advocate for broader systemic healthcare policy and practice changes. Amplify your voice by participating in advocacy campaigns or contacting legislators to champion laws that protect patient rights and healthcare professionals.

Conclusion

As you embark on this journey through the pages of this book, remember that each chapter offers knowledge and empowerment. By understanding Advance Directives, embracing the role of nurse advocacy, and responding to calls to action, you are equipped to navigate healthcare decisions with confidence and compassion. Let this book be your guide as you advocate for dignity, autonomy, and quality care in healthcare settings, inspired by the stories and strategies shared by healthcare professionals on the frontlines of patient advocacy.

Jacob Paige, R.N.

THE POEM

So live your life that the fear of death can never enter your heart. Trouble no one about their religion; respect others in their view, and demand that they respect yours. Love your life, perfect your life, beautify all things in your life. Seek to make your life long and its purpose in the service of your people. Prepare a noble death song for the day when you go over the great divide.

Always give a word or a sign of salute when meeting or passing a friend, even a stranger, when in a lonely place. Show respect to all people and grovel to none.

When you arise in the morning give thanks for the food and for the joy of living. If you see no reason for giving thanks, the fault lies only in yourself. Abuse no one and no thing, for abuse turns the wise ones to fools and robs the spirit of its vision. When it comes your time to die, be not like those whose hearts are filled with the fear of death so that when their time comes, they weep and pray for a little more time to live their lives over again in a different way. Sing your death song and die like a hero going home.

~ Chief Tecumseh

CHAPTER 1

Advance Directives

"Planning for one's death isn't about preparing for an end, but rather ensuring that the legacy of a life well lived continues to inspire and support those left behind."

The 1990 Patient Self-Determination Act (PSDA) encourages everyone to decide ahead of time about the types and extent of medical care they want to accept or refuse if they cannot make those decisions due to illness.

The PSDA requires hospitals, skilled nursing facilities, home health agencies, hospice programs, and Health Maintenance Organizations (HMOs)

- To give patients information on their state laws about their rights to make decisions about their care and to find out if patients have an advance directive.

- To recognize the advance directive and honor the patient's wishes.

- Never discriminate against patients based on whether they have filled out an advance directive or not.

Healthcare facilities can't require patients to have advance directives: It is the patient's choice.

What is an Advance Directive?

An advance directive is a legal document that explains how you want medical decisions about you to be made if you cannot make the decisions yourself. An advance directive guides your healthcare team and loved ones when they need to make these decisions or to decide who will make decisions for you when you can't. These medical decisions might include your healthcare team's actions or emergency care. An advance directive can help you think beforehand about what kind of care you want.

When filling out an advance directive, patients have several critical medical options to consider, ensuring their healthcare preferences are respected when they cannot communicate or make decisions. One of the foremost considerations is whether to receive life-sustaining treatments. These include mechanical ventilation, which helps with breathing; cardiopulmonary resuscitation (CPR) to restart the heart; and artificial nutrition and hydration provided through feeding tubes or intravenous lines. Patients can specify under which circumstances, such as terminal illness or irreversible coma, these treatments should be administered or withheld. This allows patients to avoid prolonged suffering or unwanted medical interventions that do not align with their values.

In addition to specifying life-sustaining treatments, patients can appoint a healthcare proxy or durable power of attorney for healthcare. This designated person, often a family member or close friend, is entrusted with the authority to make healthcare decisions on the patient's behalf if they become incapacitated. Selecting a healthcare proxy involves choosing someone who understands the patient's wishes and is willing to advocate for their preferences under pressure. It's also essential for the patient to have open and honest discussions with their chosen proxy to ensure they are fully informed about the patient's values and desires regarding medical treatment.

Another crucial element of an advance directive is outlining palliative and hospice care preferences. Patients can specify their wishes for pain management and comfort care, emphasizing the importance of maintaining quality of life, overextending their life in terminal situations. This can include instructions on the use of pain-relieving medications, anti-nausea treatments, and other measures to alleviate suffering and provide emotional and spiritual support. By detailing these preferences, patients can ensure they receive compassionate care focused on their comfort and dignity during the final stages of life.

Additionally, advance directives often address organ and tissue donation decisions and other post-mortem arrangements. Patients can indicate whether they wish to donate their organs and tissues for transplantation, research, or educational purposes, providing a clear directive that can be a source of comfort and clarity for surviving family members. Including these decisions in an advance directive helps ensure that the patient's end-of-life wishes are respected and that their legacy can continue in a way that aligns with their values. Overall, by thoughtfully considering and documenting these options, patients can take proactive steps to guide their healthcare journey, reduce uncertainty, and provide peace of mind for themselves and their loved ones.

Conclusion

To summarize, the 1990 Patient Self-Determination Act (PSDA) empowers individuals to take control of their healthcare decisions through advance directives. These legal tools allow patients to communicate their preferences for medical treatments, appoint a healthcare proxy, and express their wishes regarding palliative care and organ donation. By mandating that healthcare facilities provide information about these options and honor patients' decisions without discrimination, the PSDA emphasizes the significance of patient autonomy and informed consent.

Advance directives are crucial for guiding healthcare providers and loved ones in making critical medical decisions when a patient cannot do so. They help avoid unwanted medical interventions, reduce uncertainty, and offer patients and their families peace of mind. By thoughtfully considering and documenting their healthcare choices, individuals can ensure their values and wishes are respected, fostering a more compassionate and patient-centered approach to care.

CHAPTER 2

Doing my job (advocacy)

A NURSE'S ADVOCACY MEANS ACTIVELY AND CONSISTENTLY SPEAKING UP FOR A PATIENT'S NEEDS AND RESPECTING THEIR DIGNITY, GOING BEYOND JUST MEDICAL TREATMENT TO INCORPORATE COMPASSION AND ENABLE THEM TO ACTIVELY PARTICIPATE IN THEIR HEALTHCARE DECISIONS, ESSENTIALLY ACTING AS THEIR VOICE AND CHAMPION WITHIN THE HEALTHCARE SYSTEM.

As nurses, we are the strongest advocates for our patients. We constantly assess our patients and relay improving and declining information to our team: hospitalists, specialists, pharmacists, nurse practitioners, patient care techs, and charge nurses. We request medications and labs and suggest testing based on those assessments to improve patient outcomes.

We also protect our patients by using clean and sterile techniques. Cleaning wounds, IVs, drains, rooms, and beds. We give bed baths, clean them after incontinence episodes, and maintain any catheter, tube, or drain they may have. We even protect them by validating physicians and nurse practitioners regarding medication orders for type, dose, rate, and frequency.

One of our most challenging jobs in advocacy is getting family members to respect and honor their family member's wishes. Their Advance Directives, including their "Do Not Resuscitate" advance directives, are legal documents that provide instructions from your loved one for medical care, testing, and treatment. These Advance Directives only go into effect when your loved one can no longer communicate their wishes.

These documents can be particular. They can request not to do CPR, intubation, or a myriad of other options. These documents are legal in the eyes of the law because they are filled out while the patient is of sound mind, and informed consent has been provided by a physician and witnessed by a registered nurse.

Informed Consent

Informed consent is a cornerstone principle of medical ethics and patient rights in healthcare. It ensures that patients are fully aware of and understand the details of any medical procedure or surgery they are about to undergo. Informed consent is a fundamental principle embodying respect for individual autonomy and the right to make decisions about one's medical care.

Obtaining informed consent involves clear, open communication between the healthcare provider and the patient. This typically includes a detailed discussion and written materials outlining the procedure. The patient is encouraged to ask questions and express any concerns. It's crucial that the patient comprehends this information thoroughly and is competent to make the decision. Once the patient has all the necessary information and has had the opportunity to discuss it, they can voluntarily agree to or decline the procedure by signing a consent form. This ensures patients' autonomy is respected and they actively participate in their healthcare decisions. This concept gains particular significance when discussing Advance Directives and crucial documents guiding medical decisions when individuals may no longer communicate their preferences.

Imagine a scenario where Sarah, a thoughtful individual in her mid-fifties, decides to draft Advance Directives. She understands that life can be unpredictable and wishes to articulate her healthcare preferences in advance should she ever face a situation where she cannot speak for herself. Sarah's journey begins with an exploration of what informed consent truly entails.

At its core, informed consent demands that patients be adequately informed about the nature of their medical condition, the proposed treatment or procedure, its potential benefits and risks, and any alternatives available. This information empowers individuals like Sarah to make decisions aligned with their values and wishes.

As Sarah sits with her healthcare provider, she talks in-depth about her health, potential future scenarios, and what matters most to her regarding medical care. Together, they discuss various treatment options, likely outcomes, and the implications of each choice. Sarah learns that her Advance Directives will embody these preferences, serving as a guide to healthcare professionals should she be unable to communicate her wishes directly.

Through this process, Sarah recognizes the importance of clarity and specificity in her Advance Directives. She carefully outlines her preferences regarding life-sustaining treatments, such as resuscitation, ventilator use, and artificial nutrition and hydration. Sarah ensures her directives reflect her values, religious beliefs, and personal goals, ensuring that her medical care aligns with her wishes even in unforeseen circumstances.

Informed consent thus becomes a beacon of autonomy and respect in Sarah's journey. It transforms from a legal requirement into a profound affirmation of her rights and values. By understanding and articulating her wishes through Advance Directives, Sarah safeguards her autonomy and provides invaluable guidance to her loved ones and healthcare providers, ensuring that her voice continues to resonate in her medical care, even when she cannot speak for herself.

Informed consent in the context of Advance Directives encapsulates more than a legal formality—it represents an individual's empowerment to shape their healthcare journey according to their deepest values and preferences. For Sarah, this journey is not just about paperwork; it's about ensuring that her voice endures and guiding her medical care with clarity, compassion, and respect for her autonomy.

Conclusion

In the complex and emotionally charged world of healthcare, nurses serve as unwavering advocates for their patients, ensuring their voices are heard, and their wishes are respected, even in the most challenging situations. From performing meticulous assessments to coordinating with a multidisciplinary team, nurses play a vital role in safeguarding patient outcomes. They protect their patients through rigorous hygiene practices, maintaining sterile environments, and challenging medical decisions when necessary. The most difficult aspect of their advocacy is navigating the delicate balance between respecting advance directives and managing family dynamics. Nurses are entrusted with upholding the legal and ethical standards of informed consent, particularly when honoring a patient's end-of-life wishes. This commitment to patient autonomy and dignity exemplifies nurses' deep respect for the individuals in their care, ensuring that their patients' voices continue to guide their treatment, even when they can no longer speak for themselves.

CHAPTER 3.0

Unrealistic expectations

"Expectation is the root of all heartache."

- William Shakespeare.

Growing up, I loved watching medical shows. M.A.S.H., E.R. Emergency, Chicago Hope, Dougie Houser M.D., House, and Grey's Anatomy. I grew up on these shows. These were the only visuals I had in the world of medicine. They are emergently managing patient's blood pressure, inter-cranial pressure, gunshot wounds, impalement, missing limbs, and some infrequent diseases.

They are calling "CODE BLUE," someone is leaning over the patient, pushing lightly on the chest, and doing compressions. They are using the bag to breathe. The team is pushing meds, and we are always rooting for them to pull them off. I think it was in Chicago Med when they ran a code for 15 seconds and called it. Or, for dramatic effect, a show will use a cut scene panning to the clock, and someone speaks up to say they have been coding for an hour and need to call it.

At this moment, we are sitting there saying no, you can't give up. When I watch these shows, there is always that scene where someone isn't ready to give up. They keep going all by themselves. Despite the case facts, their whole team has stopped working on the patient, but they won't call it quits. A friend of the worker is trying to hold them back, but they keep pressing on. And just like any good drama, the person who would not give up gets the patient back, the patient wakes up and squeezes out a thank you or some relevant plot information.

<u>We don't have people who do that in real life.</u>

What we do have is the remarkable education and training of a Code Blue medical team. I will introduce you to some of the team next.

Conclusion

In real life, the outcomes of a "Code Blue" aren't scripted. Success relies on a finely tuned, highly trained team working with precision, communication, and extensive knowledge honed over the years. While the world of television often dramatizes these moments with lone heroes and miraculous recoveries, real-life medicine shows us the power of teamwork, expertise, and realistic care. Every person in a Code Blue team has a critical role and brings unique skills to give each patient the best possible chance.

As we step beyond the TV screen, I'd like to introduce you to the incredible professionals who work together to respond to these crises—the real-life code blue medical team. These are the people who are truly making a difference, not with last-minute heroics but with unparalleled preparation and teamwork. Let's meet the team.

CHAPTER 3.1

The team

"Medicine is a team sport. It takes the collaboration of many to provide the best patient care."

— Anonymous

When a "Code Blue" is announced in a hospital, it signals a life-threatening emergency requiring the immediate expertise of a highly educated and well-trained medical team. Here's a glimpse into the remarkable amount of education and training these professionals bring.

The Attending Physician: The Experienced Leader

The attending physician leads the team, bringing years of rigorous education and hands-on experience. Having completed medical school, a demanding residency, and often a fellowship, they possess deep knowledge and practical expertise. Their role is to make quick, informed decisions to guide the team in life-saving efforts.

The Resident: The Skilled Practitioner

Residents who have graduated from medical school and are in the midst of their specialized training play a critical role. They have already spent countless hours in clinical settings honing their skills and expanding their medical knowledge. Their education continues on the job, allowing them to handle emergencies adeptly under the guidance of the attending physician.

The Intern: The Fresh Talent

Fresh out of medical school, interns bring the latest academic knowledge and a passion for learning. They are in their first year of residency, eager to apply their extensive medical education in real-world scenarios. Under supervision, they gain invaluable experience, contributing to the team's efforts while continuing to learn and grow.

The Nurse: The Experienced Caregiver

Nurses are essential members of the Code Blue team. With rigorous training in nursing school, and often advanced degrees or certifications, they combine theoretical knowledge with practical experience. They excel in patient care, quick assessments, and coordination, ensuring all procedures run smoothly during the crisis.

The Respiratory Therapist: The Breathing Specialist

Respiratory therapists bring specialized knowledge of the respiratory system. Their education includes dedicated training in respiratory care, making them experts in managing airways and ventilation. Their skills are crucial in ensuring the patient receives adequate oxygenation during the emergency.

The Pharmacist: The Medication Expert

Pharmacists contribute their extensive understanding of medications. Their education, which includes a Doctor of Pharmacy (PharmD) degree and often post-graduate training, equips them to advise on the best pharmacological interventions. They ensure that the proper medications are administered quickly and safely.

The Paramedics: The Rapid Responders

Often the first to respond in pre-hospital settings, paramedics bring extensive emergency medical training. Their education includes rigorous coursework and hands-on experience in emergency care. They provide critical support during Code Blue situations, using their skills to stabilize patients and assist the hospital team.

In a Code Blue scenario, the convergence of these highly educated and trained professionals makes effective, coordinated care possible. Each team member's extensive education and continuous training enable them to respond swiftly and efficiently, ensuring the best possible outcomes for the patient.

Conclusion

During a Code Blue, the seamless coordination of a highly educated and trained medical team makes the difference between life and death. Each member, from the attending physician to the paramedics, brings specialized knowledge and skills honed through years of rigorous education and continuous training. Their collective expertise—working in unison—ensures that life-saving decisions and actions are executed swiftly and effectively. The power of their teamwork, underpinned by their deep commitment to patient care, makes these critical interventions successful.

CHAPTER 3.2

The team in action

Performing CPR (Cardiopulmonary Resuscitation) in a hospital setting is an intense and often violent procedure aimed at restoring circulation and breathing in a patient experiencing cardiac arrest. Here's an overview of the procedures involved, medications used, diagnostic tests performed, and potential outcomes:

CPR Procedure and Actions:

Chest Compressions: CPR begins with vigorous chest compressions to manually pump blood through the body when the heart has stopped beating effectively. These compressions are forceful and rhythmic, aiming to maintain circulation until normal heart function can be restored.

Airway Management: If the patient is not breathing or breathing ineffectively, an endotracheal tube is inserted through the mouth or nose into the trachea (intubation). This ensures a clear airway and allows mechanical ventilation to deliver oxygen and remove carbon dioxide.

Establishing Emergent Intravenous (IV) Access is crucial for rapidly administering medications and fluids that can improve the chances of survival. However, intraosseous (IO) access becomes a vital alternative when traditional IV access is difficult or time-consuming. IO access involves inserting a needle directly into the bone marrow, allowing for the quick delivery of medications into the central circulation. This method is beneficial in emergencies when veins may collapse or be inaccessible due to shock or other factors. Establishing IO access quickly and effectively can significantly improve patient outcomes during cardiac arrest.

Medications Used During CPR:

- **Epinephrine (Adrenaline):** Stimulates the heart and improves circulation during cardiac arrest.

- **Amiodarone:** Used to stabilize irregular heart rhythms (ventricular fibrillation or ventricular tachycardia) during resuscitation efforts.

- **Atropine:** Used to treat bradycardia (slow heart rate) and improve heart rate during cardiac arrest.

Diagnostic Tests:

- **Blood Gases (ABGs):** Monitors oxygenation and acid-base balance.

- **Electrolytes (e.g., potassium, calcium):** Checks for imbalances affecting heart function.

- **Cardiac Enzymes (e.g., troponin, creatine kinase):** Indicates heart muscle damage.

Intense Nature of CPR:

- **Violent Chest Compressions:** These are necessary but can cause rib fractures or damage to internal organs due to the force applied.

- **Placement of Tubes:** Endotracheal tubes are inserted for mechanical ventilation. Nasogastric tubes may also be placed to decompress the stomach and prevent aspiration (a condition in which food, liquids, saliva, or vomit is breathed into the airways).

- **Tearing of Clothes:** Rapid removal of clothing is often necessary to gain immediate access to the patient's chest for defibrillation and CPR.

- **Loss of Bodily Functions:** During cardiac arrest, patients may lose control of bodily functions due to the lack of circulation and oxygenation.

- **Use of Defibrillator:** A defibrillator delivers an electric shock to the heart to stop abnormal electrical activity (like ventricular fibrillation) and allow normal rhythm to resume.

- **Need for Blood Products:** In some cases, blood transfusions or blood products (like packed red blood cells or plasma) may be needed to replace lost blood volume or correct coagulation disorders.

The goal of CPR is to restore spontaneous circulation and breathing. Despite intensive efforts, CPR may not always be successful in resuscitating a patient. In such cases, decisions regarding the continuation of resuscitation efforts are made based on medical futility and patient wishes, including those documented in Advance Directives.

While CPR is a life-saving procedure, it is physically demanding and involves aggressive interventions aimed at restarting the heart and restoring breathing in critically ill patients experiencing cardiac arrest.

I tell you this because CPR is NOTHING like you see on TV. CPR is violent! There is nothing pleasant about it. It is not people patting your chest and speaking calmly while giving orders.

Again, it is violent. During my first code, nothing, not even what would have amounted to hours of CPR training, had prepared me for the sounds and feelings of compressing someone's chest: the popping, crunching, dislocating, and breaking of the ribs along the sternum.

It is unbelievably exhausting. Using a well-made CPR dummy was exhausting but still less tiring than performing CPR on a natural person, especially on larger individuals or more obese individuals. The organized chaos when the code team shows up is something to behold. Everyone has a job to do, and they do it well. If someone doesn't have a specific task, they are next up for chest compressions. You are so glad they are there.

Conclusion

CPR in a hospital setting is a physically demanding and emotionally intense procedure, far removed from its portrayal on television. The forceful chest compressions, airway management, and administration of life-saving medications are essential but often violent, resulting in broken ribs and other internal injuries. The organized chaos of the code team working together to restore life is exhausting and awe-inspiring, with each member playing a critical role. Despite the rigorous training, nothing can fully prepare one for the harsh reality of performing CPR on a natural person, where the ultimate goal is to bring someone back from the brink of death, even though success is never guaranteed.

CHAPTER 3.3

It's time

After all possible interventions have been applied, the team assesses the patient's response to treatment. If the patient's condition stabilizes, they are transferred to an intensive care unit for further management.

If resuscitation efforts do not yield a response, the attending physician, in consultation with the team, may make the difficult decision to terminate the Code Blue. This decision is made after careful consideration of all factors, including the duration of resuscitation and the patient's overall prognosis. Here are some considerations.

The Ethical Considerations: The Human Aspect Ethical considerations are paramount in ending a Code Blue due to death. The team must respect the patient's previously expressed wishes, such as those outlined in Advance Directives. They consider the quality of life the patient would have if resuscitation were successful, ensuring that actions taken are in the best interest of the patient's dignity and comfort.

The Collective Decision: A Unified Approach The decision to end a Code Blue is collaborative. The attending physician leads the process, but input from the entire team is crucial. Open communication and shared observations from residents, interns, nurses, respiratory therapists, and pharmacists create a comprehensive understanding of the patient's status. This collective expertise ensures the decision is thorough, compassionate, and ethically sound.

Acknowledging the Outcome: Providing Closure Once the decision to end the Code Blue is made, the team transitions to providing support and care to the family. They communicate the outcome with empathy and clarity, offering comfort and answering questions. The team focuses on honoring the patient's life and providing emotional support to loved ones.

Ending a Code Blue due to death involves profound consideration and expertise from a diverse medical team. Their combined knowledge, experience, and ethical deliberation ensure the decision is made with the utmost care, prioritizing the patient's dignity and providing compassionate closure for the family.

Conclusion

After all possible interventions have been applied, the decision to end a Code Blue is made with deep ethical consideration and a collective approach. If the patient does not respond to resuscitation efforts, the attending physician, in consultation with the entire team, must decide to terminate the Code Blue. This decision involves evaluating the patient's overall prognosis, respecting their previously expressed wishes, and considering their potential quality of life. The process is collaborative, with input from all team members—residents, interns, nurses, respiratory therapists, and pharmacists—ensuring a compassionate and well-rounded assessment. Once the decision is made, the team focuses on providing support and clear communication to the family, offering comfort and addressing their needs while honoring the patient's dignity. This process reflects the profound responsibility and care that guide medical decisions in the face of death.

Jacob Paige, R.N.

STORIES FROM THE FRONTLINE

Mary BSN- ICU Nurse 12 years

As an ICU nurse, I've encountered countless challenging situations, but one patient's story stands out vividly in my memory. Let's call him Mr. Johnson.

Mr. Johnson was a kindhearted gentleman in his late seventies, admitted to our ICU after a devastating fall at home. He had been on blood thinners for a heart condition, which compounded the severity of his injuries. Despite our best efforts, including multiple surgeries and aggressive treatment to stabilize him, his condition continued to deteriorate rapidly. The doctors informed his family that Mr. Johnson's organs were failing due to severe internal bleeding, and there was little hope of recovery.

In anticipation of such situations, Mr. Johnson had previously filled out and filed an advance directive with our hospital. In it, he explicitly stated his wishes: he did not want to be put on a ventilator, undergo CPR, or receive artificial feeding if his condition became terminal. He had discussed these decisions with his family, emphasizing his desire for a natural end if medical interventions could not restore his quality of life.

Despite his clear and legally binding wishes, tensions arose when his family arrived at the hospital. Understandably distraught and emotional, they pleaded with the doctors to do everything possible to keep Mr. Johnson alive. They questioned the advance directive, arguing that Mr. Johnson might have changed his mind in the face of such a critical situation.

I found myself in the delicate position of being both an advocate for Mr. Johnson's wishes and a source of support for his family during this agonizing time. I spent hours with them, listening to their fears and comforting them as best I could. I explained the advance directive process, emphasizing that it was designed to honor Mr. Johnson's autonomy and ensure his wishes were respected, even when he could no longer communicate them himself.

The doctors continued to provide compassionate care, managing Mr. Johnson's pain and administering medications to keep him comfortable. Despite every effort, his condition worsened, and it became clear that the next step would be placing him on a ventilator—a step directly contrary to his wishes.

Amid this heartbreaking situation, I shared stories of Mr. Johnson's life with his family—his love for gardening, his dedication to his grandchildren, and his unwavering kindness. I encouraged them to consider what Mr. Johnson would want for himself if he could speak to them now. Gradually, they began to accept that honoring his wishes was the ultimate act of love and respect they could offer him.

Eventually, the family agreed to honor Mr. Johnson's advance directive. With heavy hearts and tear-filled eyes, they made the difficult decision to transition to comfort-focused care, allowing Mr. Johnson to pass peacefully and surrounded by loved ones rather than undergo invasive interventions that would only prolong his suffering.

Mr. Johnson's story taught me the importance of Advance Directives and open communication within families. It underscored the critical role of healthcare providers in advocating for patient's wishes, even in the face of familial opposition. Most importantly, it highlighted the need for compassion and understanding during life's most challenging moments, ensuring patients' dignity and autonomy are honored until their last breath.

Amanda BSN, RN, CWS, CCRN - ICU Nurse

In my line of work, I've unfortunately witnessed many instances where families prolong the lives of their loved ones despite clear directives and medical realities. One particular case during the COVID-19 pandemic stands out vividly in my memory.

There was a patient, let's call her Mrs. Smith, who had been on a ventilator for nearly 4 weeks due to complications from COVID-19. Her condition was severe,—with kidney failure, Acute Respiratory Distress Syndrome (ARDS), and the need for prolonged prone (face down) positioning—16 to 20 hours a day. Mrs. Johnson had an advance directive meticulously outlining her wishes: no dialysis, no artificial airway, and no artificial feeding.

As Mrs. Smith's health deteriorated despite intensive medical efforts, doctors repeatedly discussed her prognosis with her husband and daughter. They emphasized that she showed no signs of improvement and continued declining. Despite these frank discussions, the family remained adamant about continuing aggressive treatments, even as Mrs. Smith's condition worsened to the point where she required dialysis and her oxygen levels plummeted despite being maxed out on the ventilator.

The situation grew increasingly tense as the family became hostile toward the medical team, including nurses and physicians, who advocated for honoring Mrs. Smith's wishes.

Jacob Paige, R.N.

Efforts to reason with the family were met with resistance, leading to the involvement of the hospital's Ethics Committee and legal advisors. Eventually, the hospital decided to withdraw care per Mrs. Smith's advance directive.

In a heart-wrenching turn of events, Mrs. Johnson's daughter's behavior escalated to the point where she had to be escorted out of the hospital, preventing her from being present during her mother's final moments. It was a stark reminder of the emotional turmoil and ethical dilemmas that arise when medical decisions conflict with deeply held familial hopes and expectations.

Mrs. Thompson was brought to the ICU after aspirating and being intubated and placed on a ventilator (a breathing machine)—a daunting situation for anyone, especially in her eighties. After a few days, she was extubated, but her respiratory challenges persisted, and she had to be re-intubated. During this time, Mrs. Thompson, alert and lucid despite her medical ordeal, had discussions with palliative care about her wishes.

She expressed her interest in a palliative care approach, seeking comfort and quality of life over aggressive treatments. However, her son and daughter strongly opposed her decision, pleading with her to continue aggressive medical interventions. Despite these conflicts, Mrs. Thompson was extubated again with plans to manage her swallowing difficulties, a consequence of lesions and tumors in her trachea and esophagus, through careful monitoring and NPO status (nil per os, meaning nothing by mouth).

Against medical advice, her family insisted on giving her sweet tea, which led to Mrs. Thompson being intubated for the third time due to aspiration. This decision marked a turning point in her treatment journey. Despite expressing her wishes for palliative care earlier, Mrs. Thompson found herself trached (a surgically created hole in your windpipe) and pegged (**p**ercutaneous **e**ndoscopic **g**astrostomy). They were placing a feeding tube through the skin and the stomach wall. She was unable to wean from the ventilator. She was transferred to a Long-Term Acute Care Hospital (LTACH). After a short time, she returned to the hospital with pneumonia, severe wounds, and deteriorating health.

Throughout her ordeal, Mrs. Thompson remained capable of communicating her profound fatigue, pain, and desire to stop the aggressive treatments. Despite these heartfelt expressions, she felt unable to confront her family's fervent insistence on continuing all medical interventions. This internal conflict took a toll, leading to severe depression, withdrawal from physical therapy, and refusal of primary care.

Mrs. Thompson spent five weeks in the ICU initially, followed by a brief stint at the LTACH and another four weeks back in the ICU. As her health declined further, she developed sepsis. The sepsis caused organ failure. She then required full pressure support (IV medications for blood pressure) and eventually coded. Despite the medical team's best efforts, Mrs. Thompson passed away.

I had a very similar situation with a post-operative open heart that failed post-op extubation. They subsequently had to be re-intubated. That did not last long, as they had to be trached and pegged. They had to be transferred to an LTACH and back to the ICU two different times over four months, eventually becoming so depressed and withdrawn that she would not even make eye contact with staff and family. Her son and daughter, despite all complications, guilted mom into continuing vent support. Finally, her sister came to visit from out of state. The sister was appalled at the patient's current condition. She was appalled because she knew her sister would never want to live like this. In talking with the sister, the son and daughter lied to her and told her that the patient was improving.

She was told her sister was doing therapy and getting better. It was a big family issue, but the sister did convince the son, daughter, and patient to go into palliative care. She survived less than thirty minutes when taken off the ventilator.

Jacob Paige, R.N.

MIRANDA, BSN, MSN

We had a patient in her early thirties, a successful dance studio owner and instructor, who was admitted to the hospital with altered mental status and malnutrition. She had recently been diagnosed with end-stage breast cancer. Despite the medical recommendation to enter hospice care, her family chose to pursue holistic healing methods, hoping for a different outcome.

During her stay, the patient required thoracentesis. This procedure involves inserting a needle into the pleural space around the lungs to remove excess fluid that can cause difficulty breathing. Although this procedure could help relieve her symptoms temporarily, we informed the family that it would not address the underlying issue of her advanced cancer. Unfortunately, her condition deteriorated rapidly, necessitating an urgent transfer to the ICU.

Upon her arrival in the ICU, the medical team quickly faced the difficult decision of whether to continue aggressive treatment, knowing that her condition was critical and that further interventions would likely be futile. Within minutes, the patient coded, and despite the family's belief in holistic medicine, they insisted on pursuing all possible life-saving measures.

The team attempted multiple times to explain the severity of the situation, emphasizing that the patient's metastatic breast cancer had spread to her bones and that any further resuscitation efforts would not change the inevitable outcome. However, the family could not accept this reality and insisted that we continue for an hour and seventeen minutes.

The absence of an advance directive or a designated healthcare power of attorney complicated the situation. This meant that all family members were involved in making decisions about her care, making it incredibly challenging for the team to provide appropriate and compassionate care.

As nurses, we are taught to do no harm, but it felt like we were doing the opposite in this situation. The family's unrealistic expectations made an already heartbreaking scenario even more difficult. The fact that the patient was young and had so much life ahead of her made it even harder for the staff, who could easily relate to her. She had been unconscious for days, and her emaciated state made it clear that she was no longer truly present. Yet, despite our repeated explanations, the family continued to urge us to do more.

Despite the efforts of physicians, chaplains, nurses, and leadership, the family could not come to terms with the severity of her illness. Eventually, the patient passed away, finally finding peace. However, the experience left a profound impact on our staff. We held a debriefing session a few days later, attended by day and night shift nurses, physicians, chaplains, pharmacists, medical students, and nursing leadership. This allowed us to process the situation together, but this patient's memory lingers in our minds. The traumatic nature of the events has made it impossible to forget.

CHAPTER 4

The Toll it takes

"We don't always get to choose the roles we play in life, but we do have to live with the impact those roles have on our soul."

— Anonymous

Running a Code Blue is a high-stakes event when every second counts, and every action can mean the difference between life and death. For the medical team involved particularly nurses—it demands technical precision and emotional resilience. However, the intense pressure and the weight of the responsibility can take a significant mental toll on those who are frequently called to respond.

The Immediate Adrenaline Rush

When the Code Blue alarm sounds, there's an instant surge of adrenaline. Nurses, doctors, and other members of the code team spring into action. Their training is kicking in as they race to the patient's side. In these moments, the focus is on starting compressions, securing airways, administering medications, and coordinating the team. The flurry of activity is intense, and everyone is acutely aware that they are fighting against time.

This adrenaline rush serves a purpose—it heightens alertness and sharpens decision-making. However, the body is not designed to sustain this stress level indefinitely. The immediate aftermath of a Code Blue, whether the patient survives or not, often leaves the team members drained, their bodies still flooded with stress hormones.

Emotional Whiplash

The emotional impact of running a Code Blue can be profound and varied. When a patient is resuscitated, there is a collective sense of relief and achievement. But this relief is often fleeting, replaced by the sobering realization that the patient's future is still uncertain. For many, the question lingers: "Did we just prolong the inevitable?"

When efforts to revive the patient fail, the emotional toll can be even heavier. Nurses, who often have the most direct and prolonged contact with patients, may feel a deep sense of loss, even if they try to remain emotionally detached. The clinical setting does little to shield them from the human reality of death. Despite their best efforts, seeing a life slip away can evoke feelings of helplessness and frustration.

For some, this experience can trigger a sense of guilt. They may question their actions during the code: "Did I push hard enough during compressions?" "Did I miss something critical?" This self-doubt can be corrosive, affecting their confidence and mental well-being.

The Burden of Repetition

The toll of running Code Blues is not limited to isolated events; it accumulates over time. Nurses in critical care settings where codes are more frequent may find themselves repeatedly exposed to traumatic situations. The human brain is not wired to witness so much death and suffering without consequence.

Over time, this can lead to emotional exhaustion where compassion fatigue sets in.

Compassion fatigue is particularly insidious because it can erode a nurse's ability to connect with patients and colleagues, leading to isolation. Constant exposure to trauma can also lead to burnout, where the emotional and physical demands of the job become overwhelming. Nurses may start feeling numb or detached from their work and personal lives.

The Psychological Impact

Beyond burnout and compassion fatigue, frequent involvement in Code Blues can contribute to more serious mental health issues. Post-traumatic stress disorder (PTSD) is not uncommon among healthcare workers who are regularly exposed to life-threatening situations. The symptoms of PTSD—nightmares, flashbacks, and hyper-vigilance—can be debilitating, affecting both professional performance and personal relationships.

Moreover, the culture of stoicism that often pervades healthcare can make it difficult for nurses and other core team members to seek help. There is a pervasive expectation to "power through" and remain resilient, even in the face of overwhelming stress. This can lead to the suppression of emotions, intensifying the psychological burden.

The Weight of Prolonging the Inevitable

One of the most emotionally taxing aspects of running a Code Blue occurs when the patient is clearly at the end of life but the family is not ready to let go. The medical team is often caught in a heartbreaking dilemma in these situations. They know that the patient's body is beyond the point of recovery, that continuing aggressive interventions will not change the outcome, and that in some cases it may even cause unnecessary suffering. Yet, they must balance this clinical reality with the family's wishes, which may be driven by hope, denial, or a deep-seated fear of loss.

Jacob Paige, R.N.

Performing a complete code on a patient who is ready to leave this world but whose family insists on more and more being done can take a profound mental toll on the team. Every round of chest compressions, every dose of medication, and every attempt to revive a fading heartbeat feels increasingly futile, and the emotional weight of these actions can be overwhelming.

Nurses and doctors may feel like they are inflicting more harm than good, violating the core principle of do no harm. The distress is compounded by the visible signs of the patient's suffering—bruised ribs from compressions, the vacant look in the eyes of someone who is no longer truly present, and the labored gasps from a ventilator. Each additional measure taken at the family's request can feel like an extension of the patient's agony rather than an effort to save a life.

The mental toll is not just about the physical acts involved in the code; it's also about the ethical and emotional burden. Healthcare providers often struggle with the knowledge that they are prolonging the inevitable, possibly at the cost of the patient's dignity. They are keenly aware of the fine line between life-sustaining treatment and the mere prolongation of death, and being forced to cross that line can leave deep emotional scars.

For the team, these experiences can lead to moral distress—a state in which they know the ethically appropriate action to take but cannot act on it due to external pressures, such as the family's wishes. This moral distress can be deeply unsettling, leading to feelings of powerlessness, frustration, and guilt. Over time, repeated exposure to such situations can erode the emotional resilience of even the most experienced healthcare providers, contributing to burnout, compassion fatigue, and long-term psychological harm.

Coping Mechanisms and Support

Despite the challenges, there are ways to mitigate the mental toll of running Code Blues. Debriefings after a code, where the team can discuss what happened, are crucial. These sessions provide an opportunity to process the events, share emotions, and offer support to one another. They also help identify what went well and what could be improved, alleviating some of the guilt and self-doubt that might arise.

Peer support is another vital resource. Nurses and other healthcare workers who understand the unique stresses of the job can offer empathy and solidarity. Formal support systems, such as counseling and mental health services, should also be readily available and encouraged by healthcare institutions.

Some nurses find that maintaining a strong sense of purpose and meaning in their work helps to buffer the emotional strain. Remembering why they chose this profession in the first place—whether it was the desire to help others, the fulfillment of making a difference, or the commitment to patient care—can provide a powerful counterbalance to the mental toll.

The Need for Systemic Change

Addressing the mental toll of running Code Blues requires systemic changes in the healthcare environment. This includes ensuring adequate staffing levels so that the burden of frequent codes does not fall disproportionately on a few individuals. It also means fostering a culture where mental health is prioritized, and nurses and other healthcare workers feel safe expressing their vulnerabilities and seeking help when needed.

Healthcare institutions must recognize that their staff's emotional and psychological well-being is not a luxury—it is a necessity. When nurses and other code team members are supported, they are better equipped to provide the compassionate, high-quality care that patients need, even in the most critical moments.

Conclusion

Running a Code Blue is one of healthcare's most challenging aspects. The immediate rush of adrenaline, the emotional rollercoaster, and the long-term psychological impact can significantly impact nurses and the rest of the code team. The weight of prolonging life when a patient is ready to leave this world but the family is not adds a layer of emotional complexity that can be deeply distressing. While individual coping mechanisms and support systems are essential, there is a pressing need for broader changes within the healthcare system to address and mitigate this mental burden. Only by acknowledging and addressing these challenges can we ensure that those who save lives can also preserve their well-being.

CHAPTER 4.5

The Legal dilemma: physicians, Advance Directives, and the fear of lawsuits

"Frivolous lawsuits create an environment of defensive medicine, where doctors order unnecessary tests and procedures out of fear of litigation rather than the patient's best interest."

-Richard J. Roberts, Nobel Laureate in Medicine.

End-of-life scenarios offer a significant challenge when physicians face pressure from a patient's Medical Durable Power of Attorney (DPOA) to overturn Advance Directives. The fear of potential lawsuits from surviving family members often influences these decisions, creating a complex and ethically fraught situation for healthcare providers.

Advance Directives guide physicians in providing care that aligns with the patient's values.

A Medical Durable Power of Attorney (DPOA) is a person the patient appoints to make healthcare decisions if they cannot do so. The DPOA is expected to honor the patient's wishes outlined in their Advance Directives. However, in practice, situations often arise where the DPOA's decisions conflict with the patient's documented preferences, leading to ethical and legal dilemmas for physicians.

One of the primary concerns for physicians in these situations is the potential for lawsuits from surviving family members. When a patient passes away, family members who disagree with the patient's Advance Directives or the decisions made by the DPOA may threaten or pursue legal action against the healthcare providers involved. This fear of litigation can significantly influence physicians' decisions, leading them to override Advance Directives to avoid potential legal repercussions.

"The dead can't sue."

- Unknown

Case Studies and Real-Life Scenarios

Consider the case of Mrs. J, an 85-year-old woman with a DNR order and Advance Directives clearly stating that she did not want to be kept alive on mechanical ventilation. Her DPOA, her son, was adamant that everything possible be done to save her life when she suffered a severe stroke. The attending physician faced an immediate ethical and legal conflict: honor Mrs. J's wishes as documented in her Advance Directives or comply with her son's demands to avoid the risk of a lawsuit.

Ultimately, the physician followed the son's instructions, fearing legal consequences for the family. Mrs. J was placed on a ventilator and underwent aggressive treatment, contrary to her stated wishes. This case highlights the profound impact of the fear of litigation on medical decision-making, often leading to outcomes that are misaligned with the patient's desires.

There is an ethical and emotional toll on physicians who find themselves in these situations and often experience significant ethical distress. They are torn between their professional obligation to honor the patient's wishes and the legal pressure to comply with the family's demands. This conflict can lead to moral injury, a condition where the healthcare provider's sense of right and wrong is compromised, resulting in emotional and psychological distress.

Moreover, these scenarios can erode the trust between healthcare providers and patients. When Advance Directives are not honored, it undermines the integrity of the patient's autonomy and can lead to a broader mistrust of the healthcare system among patients and their families.

How do we continue navigating the legal landscape to address these challenges? Healthcare providers and institutions must navigate a complex legal landscape. Legal protections for honoring Advance Directives vary by jurisdiction, and physicians must be well-versed in their region's laws governing end-of-life care. Institutions can support their medical staff by providing clear guidelines and legal counsel to help physicians make informed decisions that balance ethical obligations with legal considerations.

Effective communication and mediation are crucial in resolving conflicts between Advance Directives and the demands of the DPOA or family members. Early and ongoing discussions with patients and their families about the importance of Advance Directives and the role of the DPOA can help clarify expectations and reduce the likelihood of disputes. In cases where conflicts arise, involving ethics committees or mediators can provide a structured approach to finding a resolution that respects the patient's wishes and addresses the family's concerns.

Physicians face challenging and often scary decisions when Advance Directives are contested by a patient's Medical DPOA or family members. The fear of lawsuits from surviving family members can lead to decisions that override the patient's documented wishes, resulting in ethical and emotional turmoil for healthcare providers. By understanding the legal context, enhancing communication, and employing mediation strategies, physicians and healthcare institutions can better navigate these complex situations and ensure patient autonomy is respected and upheld.

Conclusion

End-of-life scenarios involving Advance Directives and Medical Durable Power of Attorney (DPOA) present profound challenges for physicians, who often face intense pressure from family members to override the patient's documented wishes. When the DPOA's decisions conflict with the patient's Advance Directives, healthcare providers must navigate a complex landscape influenced by the fear of potential lawsuits from surviving family members. This legal concern can lead to decisions that contradict the patient's desires, creating significant ethical and emotional distress for the medical team. The case of Mrs. J, where the attending physician opted to follow the DPOA's demands despite clear directives, underscores how litigation fears can disrupt the alignment between patient autonomy and medical practice. Addressing these challenges requires balancing legal awareness, effective communication, and mediation to ensure patient wishes are honored while managing familial and legal pressures. By fostering open dialogues and utilizing ethical committees, healthcare providers can better navigate these dilemmas, striving to uphold patient dignity and trust in the healthcare system.

CHAPTER 5

Understanding Palliative Care

"In palliative care, we aim to support the whole person, addressing their physical, emotional, and spiritual needs."

— Dame Cicely Saunders, founder of the modern hospice movement

Palliative care is a specialized approach to healthcare that focuses on improving the quality of life for patients facing serious illnesses. It is a holistic form of care that addresses not only the physical symptoms of the disease but also the emotional, social, and spiritual aspects of patient well-being. This chapter explores what palliative care entails, its goals, and how it is intended to be used.

What is Palliative Care?

Palliative care is provided by a team of healthcare professionals, including doctors, nurses, social workers, chaplains, and other specialists. Its primary goal is to enhance the quality of life for patients and their families facing the challenges associated with severe illnesses. Palliative care is appropriate at any stage of an illness, regardless of whether the patient is receiving curative treatment.

Goals of Palliative Care:

1. <u>Relief of Symptoms:</u> Palliative care focuses on managing pain, nausea, fatigue, shortness of breath, and others that may accompany serious illnesses. By addressing these symptoms, patients can experience improved comfort and overall well-being.

2. <u>Enhanced Quality of Life:</u> Beyond symptom management, palliative care supports patients in maintaining their dignity, autonomy, and emotional well-being. It helps patients and families navigate the complexities of their illness, providing them with the support and resources they need to cope effectively.

3. <u>Communication and Decision-Making:</u> Palliative care encourages open and honest communication about goals of care, treatment options, and end-of-life preferences. It facilitates discussions between patients, families, and healthcare providers to ensure that care aligns with the patient's values and wishes.

4. <u>Coordination of Care:</u> Palliative care teams collaborate closely with other healthcare providers involved in the patient's treatment, ensuring seamless transitions between settings and continuity of care. This interdisciplinary approach helps address the diverse needs of patients and their families comprehensively.

When is Palliative Care Used?

Palliative care is appropriate for patients with serious illnesses such as cancer, heart disease, chronic obstructive pulmonary disease (COPD), kidney failure, dementia, and others. It can be initiated at any point in the disease trajectory, from diagnosis onward, and provided alongside curative treatments.

Conclusion

Palliative care is a compassionate approach to healthcare that prioritizes the comfort, dignity, and overall well-being of patients facing serious illnesses. By addressing physical symptoms, providing emotional support, facilitating communication, and promoting informed decision-making, palliative care empowers patients and families to navigate challenging healthcare decisions with greater clarity and peace of mind. It underscores the importance of personalized care that respects individual values and preferences, ensuring that each patient's journey is supported with dignity and compassion.

CHAPTER 6

Understanding Hospice Care

Hospice care is a specialized form of healthcare that focuses on providing comfort and support to patients nearing the end of life. This chapter delves into what hospice care entails, its goals, and how it is intended to enhance the quality of life for patients and their families during the final stages of illness.

What is Hospice Care?

Hospice care is a compassionate approach to end-of-life care that emphasizes comfort, dignity, and quality of life for patients with terminal illnesses. It is provided by a team of healthcare professionals, including doctors, nurses, social workers, chaplains, and trained volunteers. Hospice care is generally provided in the patient's home but can also be administered in hospitals, nursing homes, or dedicated hospice facilities.

Goals of Hospice Care:

1. <u>Comfort and Symptom Management:</u> Hospice care's primary focus is managing symptoms such as pain, nausea, breathing difficulties, and others that can cause discomfort in the final stages of life. By effectively controlling symptoms, hospice care aims to improve the patient's quality of life and relieve distressing symptoms.

2. <u>Emotional and Spiritual Support:</u> Hospice care addresses patients' and their families' emotional, social, and spiritual needs. It provides counseling, support groups, and spiritual guidance to help patients and families cope with the challenges of terminal illness and impending loss.

3. <u>Quality of Life:</u> Hospice care aims to maintain or enhance the patient's quality of life by promoting dignity, autonomy, and personal choices. It respects the patient's preferences and values, ensuring that care is aligned with their wishes for comfort and peace in their final days.

4. <u>Family Support and Education:</u> Hospice care provides practical and emotional support to family caregivers, helping them navigate the complexities of caregiving and bereavement. It offers education about the dying process, anticipatory grief, and practical tips for caring for a loved one at home.

When is Hospice Care Used?

Hospice care is typically recommended when curative treatments are no longer effective or desired by the patient. It is appropriate for patients with a terminal illness or a life expectancy of six months or less, as determined by a physician's prognosis. Hospice care can be initiated at any point during the terminal phase of illness, allowing patients and families to receive comprehensive support and comfort-focused care.

So What's The Difference

How Hospice Care Differs from Palliative Care:

While hospice care and palliative care share similar goals of enhancing comfort and quality of life, they differ primarily in their timing and scope:

<u>Hospice Care:</u> designed for patients with terminal illnesses or a prognosis of six months or less. It focuses exclusively on comfort and quality of life in the final stages, often in the patient's home environment.

<u>Palliative Care:</u> Provided at any stage of a severe illness, including those receiving curative treatments. It aims to improve quality of life by addressing symptoms and supporting patients and families in making informed healthcare decisions.

Conclusion

Hospice care provides compassionate and holistic support to patients and families facing the challenges of terminal illness. It empowers patients to live their final days with peace and fulfillment by prioritizing comfort, dignity, and emotional well-being. Hospice care emphasizes personalized care that respects patients' wishes and values, ensuring a dignified and compassionate end-of-life experience. Hospice care underscores the importance of compassionate caregiving, effective symptom management, and meaningful support for patients and families navigating the end of life.

CHAPTER 7

Subjective thoughts from those who do

Tessa, RN. ICU Rapid Response Team

It was challenging to articulate this! Without using too many curse words, I couldn't type as much as I wanted. After many years, these types of patients blur together because it's all the same routine. I've observed that each state has different laws regarding DPOA and next of kin, which are like opinions—everyone has one, and everyone thinks theirs is superior!

As a nurse, your primary duty is to do no harm. With over 16 years of experience in the ICU, I encounter numerous gray areas when discussing with patients and families their preferences if their hearts were to stop. The decision boils down to resuscitation or not: DNR/DNI involves forcefully compressing a patient's chest, breaking ribs and sternum, to circulate blood adequately in hopes of sustaining brain and organ function. To insert a breathing tube to assist with breathing. To administer medications intravenously to maintain life. This is what constitutes life support.

It's challenging to believe patients and families grasp the gravity of this decision unless they have medical knowledge comparable to that of a healthcare professional. Physicians need the freedom to guide these decisions without undue legal concerns. Just as you would appoint a lawyer to represent you legally, shouldn't doctors be entrusted to make these critical healthcare decisions rather than families who lack medical expertise? I believe physicians require more support to make decisions that align with a patient's prognosis when survival is unlikely. Current legal frameworks often fall short in supporting physicians, and there should be provisions for hospital ethics teams with medical expertise to assist in such decisions legally.

As a nurse, when you inquire about a patient's code status, I've witnessed too many instances where a patient chooses DNR/DNI, only for their family to reverse that decision once the patient cannot decide for themselves. As a nurse, you invest your time, sweat, tears, fears, and anxieties in doing everything possible to save the patient by performing traumatic CPR, intubations, dialysis, emergency procedures, administering medications, and dialysis, all constituting artificial life support. Families often assert that "it was their time" or "they wouldn't want to be on life support" without fully comprehending the implications. This can result in a patient being left in a vegetative state with no quality of life while families insist on continuing treatment.

As a nurse, you contemplate the balance between Quality of Life and Quantity of Life. Wouldn't you prefer quality over quantity with the time you have? It leaves you questioning: Did I indeed do no harm?

CHAPTER 8

The Importance of Having a Difficult Conversation

"One of the most sincere forms of respect is actually listening to what another has to say."

- Bryant H. McGill

In the busyness of life, there's one conversation many of us tend to avoid: the conversation about our wishes for medical care if we were ever unable to speak for ourselves. It's not an easy topic to broach—after all, who wants to contemplate their mortality or the possibility of being incapacitated? However, having this conversation and putting your wishes in writing through an advance directive is one of the most responsible and caring actions you can take for yourself and your loved ones.

Why Have the Conversation?

Imagine a scenario where you are suddenly hospitalized due to a severe illness or injury. Your loved ones are left to make critical decisions about your medical care, unsure of what you would have wanted. This situation is emotionally taxing and can lead to disagreements among family members when unity is most needed. By discussing your wishes in advance, you relieve your loved ones of the burden of guessing your desires and empower them to advocate for you according to your preferences.

What is an Advance Directive?

An advance directive, also known as a living will, outlines your preferences for medical treatments and life-saving measures in case you cannot communicate your wishes. It covers scenarios such as whether you would want to be resuscitated, placed on life support, or receive specific treatments under certain conditions. This legal document ensures that healthcare providers and family members know and respect your healthcare preferences.

Taking Action

Having the conversation is just the first step. After discussing your wishes with your loved ones, it's crucial to formalize them by completing an advance directive document. Your healthcare provider can assist you in preparing this document, which should be kept on file with your medical records and shared with your designated healthcare proxy or family members.

Advocating for Legal Protection

In addition to taking personal responsibility, it's important to advocate for broader legal protections. Contact your local congressperson and urge them to support legislation that protects healthcare providers and facilities from legal repercussions when they honor Advance Directives. This legal protection ensures that medical professionals can respect your wishes without fear of liability, upholding your autonomy and dignity even in critical medical situations. You can find your representative on this government website:

https://www.house.gov/representatives

Conclusion

Having a difficult conversation about Advance Directives is an act of love and responsibility towards yourself and your loved ones. It ensures your voice is heard when you cannot speak for yourself in healthcare matters. By taking proactive steps—discussing your wishes, completing an advance directive, and advocating for legal protections—you safeguard your interests and contribute to a more compassionate and informed healthcare system for everyone.

Please don't wait until it's too late. Start the conversation today and take concrete steps toward securing your future healthcare preferences. Your proactive approach will provide you and your loved ones peace of mind in the face of uncertainty.

THE CHECKLIST

- Have a conversation with your loved ones.

- Have an in-depth conversation with your primary care physician.

- Fill out your Advance Directives.

- File your Advance Directives with your local healthcare facility. Keep copies in a safe place that your loved ones have access to. (They don't do us any good locked in a safe that no one can open.)

- Write your congressperson and call for legislation protecting healthcare providers when they uphold your advance directives with your wants and wishes.

- Say I love you sincerely and often.

- Know that you are easing the responsibility and tough decisions off of your loved ones.

Below is a copy of the letter I sent my Congressman Sam Graves.

Dear Congressman Graves,

I hope this letter finds you well. I am writing to you as a concerned constituent and healthcare advocate in Missouri, seeking your support for critical legislation to protect healthcare providers who honor the Advance Directives of their patients.

As you know, Advance Directives are vital documents that ensure a patient's wishes regarding their medical care are respected, particularly in end-of-life situations. These directives, including living wills and do-not-resuscitate (DNR) orders, are carefully considered by patients and should be upheld to maintain their autonomy and dignity.

However, there is a growing concern among healthcare providers about the potential legal repercussions when they honor these directives against the wishes of a patient's Medical Durable Power of Attorney (DPOA). When family members override the patient's documented desires, physicians and other medical staff often face the threat of lawsuits, which creates a significant ethical and legal dilemma. This fear can compel providers to act against the patient's wishes, resulting in unnecessary procedures and prolonged suffering.

To address this issue, I urge you to introduce and support legislation that provides legal protections for healthcare providers who follow Advance Directives, even when there is opposition from a patient's DPOA. This legislation would:

1. Affirm the Primacy of Advance Directives: Clearly state that a patient's Advance Directives should take precedence over conflicting demands from a DPOA or family members.

Jacob Paige, R.N.

2. Provide Legal Immunity: Grant healthcare providers immunity from civil liability when they act in good faith to uphold a patient's Advance Directives.

3. Establish Clear Guidelines: Create clear, uniform guidelines for healthcare providers to follow when Advance Directives are contested, ensuring they can make decisions based on the patient's documented wishes without fear of legal repercussions.

Such legislation would empower healthcare providers to honor their ethical duty to respect patient autonomy while reducing the practice of defensive medicine. It would also provide clarity and reassurance to families about the importance of respecting their loved one's expressed wishes.

As your constituent, I believe that protecting the rights of patients and supporting our healthcare providers are of utmost importance. By championing this cause, you can help ensure that patients' end-of-life wishes are respected and that healthcare providers can perform their duties without the looming threat of frivolous lawsuits.

Thank you for considering this urgent matter. I am confident that, with your support, we can create a healthcare environment that honors patient autonomy and supports our dedicated medical professionals. Please feel free to contact me at 816-***-**** or jpthern@gmail.com if you would like to discuss this issue further.

Sincerely,

Jacob Paige RN

Address:

Phone:

Email:

Unrealistic expectations

The recognition and specific regulations regarding Advance Directives can vary from state to state in the United States. Here's a general overview based on standard practices:

States that Generally Honor Advance Directives:

Alabama	Louisiana
Alaska	Maine
Arizona	Maryland
Arkansas	Massachusetts
California	Michigan
Colorado	Minnesota
Connecticut	Mississippi
Delaware	Missouri
Florida	Montana
Georgia	Nebraska
Hawaii	Nevada
Idaho	New Hampshire
Illinois	New Jersey
Indiana	New Mexico
Iowa	New York
Kansas	North Carolina
Kentucky	North Dakota

Ohio	Texas
Oklahoma	Utah
Oregon	Vermont
Pennsylvania	Virginia
Rhode Island	Washington
South Carolina	West Virginia
South Dakota	Wisconsin
Tennessee	Wyoming

States with Specific Requirements or Variations

Some states may have specific regulations or variations in how Advance Directives are recognized or interpreted.

Reviewing state-specific laws or consulting with legal professionals for detailed information is essential.

States with Limited Recognition or Specific Requirements:

1. Connecticut (requires that an attending physician and a second physician certify in writing that a patient is incapacitated).

2. Massachusetts (may require specific forms or additional documentation).

3. New Hampshire (requires the directive to be signed by two witnesses or notarized).

4. Utah (may require specific forms or additional documentation).

States with Limited or No Information Available:

For some states, detailed information on advance directive recognition may be limited or require further research.

Federal Law and Recognition:

Under federal law, Advance Directives are generally recognized across states due to the Patient Self-Determination Act (PSDA), which requires healthcare providers to inform patients about their rights to make decisions concerning medical care, including the right to execute Advance Directives.

Consultation and Legal Advice:

Given the complexities and variations in state laws regarding Advance Directives, individuals are advised to consult with legal professionals or healthcare providers to ensure compliance with state-specific requirements and to clarify any questions or concerns related to Advance Directives.

How to find advance directive specialists in each state:

1. **State Bar Association**: Each state's bar association typically offers resources and referrals to attorneys specializing in healthcare law or Advance Directives. You can visit the website of your state's bar association or contact them directly for a referral.

2. **Local Hospitals and Healthcare Providers**: Many hospitals have social workers or patient advocates who

can provide information on Advance Directives and may be able to refer you to specialists in your area.

3. **Legal Aid Organizations**: Non-profit legal aid organizations often provide free or low-cost legal services and may have attorneys specializing in healthcare law, including Advance Directives.

4. **Elder Law Attorneys**: Attorneys specializing in elder law often handle matters related to Advance Directives. They can be located through directories like the National Academy of Elder Law Attorneys (NAELA).

5. **Online Directories**: Websites like Avvo, LegalZoom, or Justia allow you to search for attorneys by practice area and location. Always verify credentials and reviews before choosing an attorney.

6. **Referrals**: Ask friends, family members, or healthcare providers for recommendations. Personal referrals can provide insights into an attorney's expertise and bedside manner.

When contacting an attorney or specialist, it's important to discuss your specific needs, including any preferences or concerns you have regarding Advance Directives. They can help you navigate the legal requirements and ensure your directives are legally sound and aligned with your wishes.

Support Groups

You can search for these groups on Facebook and similar sites.

To find relevant Facebook groups:

- Use Facebook's search feature and enter keywords like "Advance Directives," "advanced care planning," "living will," or "end-of-life care."

- Review group descriptions and membership to ensure they align with your interests and needs.

- Join groups that provide supportive and informative discussions, respecting privacy and confidentiality when sharing personal information.

Always verify the credibility and moderation of groups before actively participating or sharing personal information. These groups can provide valuable support, resources, and advanced care planning and directives discussions.

1. **Advance Care Planning (ACP) Groups**: Look for groups specifically focused on advance care planning, where members discuss topics related to Advance Directives, living wills, healthcare proxies, and end-of-life care decisions.

2. **Elder Care and Support Groups**: Groups that cater to caregivers, family members, and individuals interested in elder care often discuss Advance Directives as part of broader discussions on healthcare planning.

3. **Patient Advocacy and Rights Groups**: Some advocacy groups focus on patient rights and empower individuals to make informed decisions about their medical care, including using Advance Directives.

4. **Medical and Healthcare Professionals Groups**: Groups for healthcare providers, nurses, social workers, and medical professionals may include discussions on

best practices for advanced care planning and directive implementation.

5. **Community and Support Groups**: Local community groups or support networks may touch upon Advance Directives as part of broader discussions on healthcare and well-being.

Dear Friends,

Thank you for taking the time to explore this book and deepen your understanding of advance directives. Your commitment to educating yourself about these critical healthcare decisions empowers you and contributes to a broader culture of patient autonomy and informed consent. You are now better equipped to make informed decisions and guide others in navigating these critical conversations.

I encourage you to take the next step by reaching out to your members of Congress and advocating for policies that protect and expand individuals' rights to make their own healthcare decisions and protect the healthcare workers who honor those wishes. Your voice can help ensure everyone can access the information and resources needed to create advance directives reflecting their values and wishes.

Finally, I urge you to talk with your loved ones and take the time to set up your advance directives. By doing so, you will not only protect your wishes but also provide clarity and peace of mind for your family. Thank you for being proactive in your healthcare journey and contributing to a more compassionate and patient-centered approach to medical care.

Warm regards,

JP

ABOUT THE AUTHOR

Jacob Paige RN—I'm just a nurse. For years, I have had the privilege of working in many departments with some of the best. These departments are the Cardiac Catheter Lab, Electrophysiology Lab, PACU, Neuro/ Tele, med surg/Tele, Cardiac Step-down, EVS, and central supply (the last two were when they cut hours and procedures during COVID-19).

I have worked with some of the most brilliant, dedicated, compassionate, caring, and overworked people I have ever met. I have seen a lot of people in all levels of medical needs. Sadly I have seen too many patients who were ready to leave this world get stuck in the hospital for a few more minutes, hours, days, or weeks because family members didn't respect their wishes. Family members who didn't understand the gravity of the situation and weren't ready to say goodbye. Hence... This Book

www.ingramcontent.com/pod-product-compliance
Lightning Source LLC
Chambersburg PA
CBHW070206230526
45471CB00002B/841